Great Lies To Tell Small Kids

Andy Riley is the author of *THE BOOK OF BUNNY SUICIDES* and *RETURN OF THE BUNNY SUICIDES*. He has written for *Black Books*, *Little Britain*, *Smack The Pony*, *Trigger Happy TV*, *Big Train* and *The Armando Iannucci Shows*. He is the co-creator of *Hyperdrive*, BBC2's new science fiction sitcom, and Radio 4's *The 99p Challenge*. His weekly cartoon strip, *Roasted*, runs in the *Observer Magazine*.

Great Lies To Tell Small Kids

Andy Riley

A PLUME BOOK

PLUME
Published by Penguin Group
Penguin Group (USA) Inc., 375 Hudson Street, New York, New York 10014, U.S.A.
Penguin Group (Canada), 90 Eglinton Avenue East, Suite 700, Toronto, Ontario, Canada M4P 2Y3 (a division of Pearson Penguin Canada Inc.)
Penguin Books Ltd., 80 Strand, London WC2R 0RL, England
Penguin Ireland, 25 St. Stephen's Green, Dublin 2, Ireland (a division of Penguin Books Ltd.)
Penguin Group (Australia), 250 Camberwell Road, Camberwell, Victoria 3124, Australia (a division of Pearson Australia Group Pty. Ltd.)
Penguin Books India Pvt. Ltd., 11 Community Centre, Panchsheel Park, New Delhi – 110 017, India
Penguin Books (NZ), cnr Airborne and Rosedale Roads, Albany, Auckland 1310, New Zealand (a division of Pearson New Zealand Ltd.)
Penguin Books (South Africa) (Pty.) Ltd., 24 Sturdee Avenue, Rosebank, Johannesburg 2196, South Africa

Penguin Books Ltd., Registered Offices: 80 Strand, London WC2R 0RL, England

Published by Plume, a member of Penguin Group (USA) Inc. Originally published in Great Britain by Hodder & Stoughton.

First American Printing, February 2006
10 9 8 7 6 5 4 3 2 1

Copyright © Andy Riley, 2005
All rights reserved

℗ REGISTERED TRADEMARK—MARCA REGISTRADA

CIP data is available.
ISBN 0-452-28624-7

Printed in the United States of America

BOOKS ARE AVAILABLE AT QUANTITY DISCOUNTS WHEN USED TO PROMOTE PRODUCTS OR SERVICES. FOR INFORMATION PLEASE WRITE TO PREMIUM MARKETING DIVISION, PENGUIN GROUP (USA) INC., 375 HUDSON STREET, NEW YORK, NEW YORK 10014.

With thanks to:
Polly Faber, Camilla Hornby, Kevin Cecil,
Trena Keating & Emily Haynes & all at Plume,
Nick Davies & all at Hodder

Rain is Jesus's wee-wee

THERE'S NO SUCH THING AS KANGAROOS
THEY'RE JUST MICE STANDING VERY NEAR

WINE

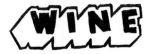

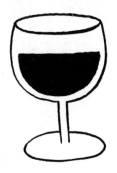

MAKES MOMMY
CLEVER

POLICEMEN GROW FROM HELMETS IN A SINGLE NIGHT

IT'S UNLUCKY NOT TO NAME EVERY ANT YOU SEE

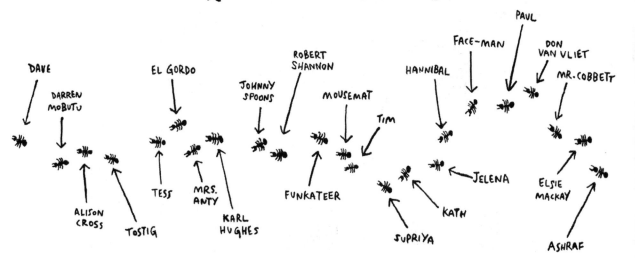

DAVE

DARREN MOBUTU

ALISON CROSS

TOSTIG

EL GORDO

TESS

MRS. ANTY

KARL HUGHES

JOHNNY SPOONS

ROBERT SHANNON

MOUSEMAT

TIM

FUNKATEER

HANNIBAL

FACE-MAN

PAUL

DON VAN VLIET

MR. COBBETT

JELENA

KATH

SUPRIYA

ELSIE MACKAY

ASHRAF

FOR YOUR WHOLE LIFE

WHEN YOU LEAVE THE ROOM,
COOKED SPAGHETTI TRIES TO
WRIGGLE BACK HOME TO ITALY

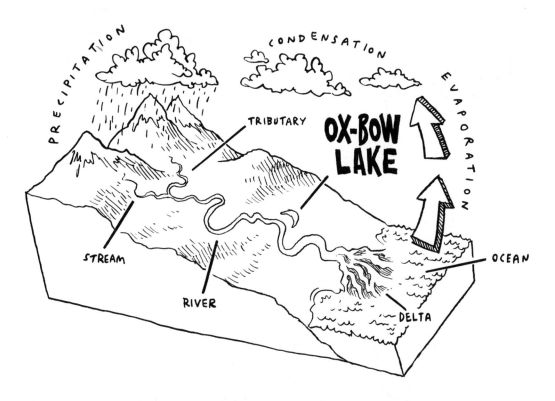

WHEN THEY TEACH YOU THE WATER CYCLE AT SCHOOL, MAKE SURE YOU REMEMBER THE BIT ABOUT **OX-BOW LAKES.** YOU'LL COME ACROSS THEM A **LOT** IN LATER LIFE.

MILK FEELS PAIN

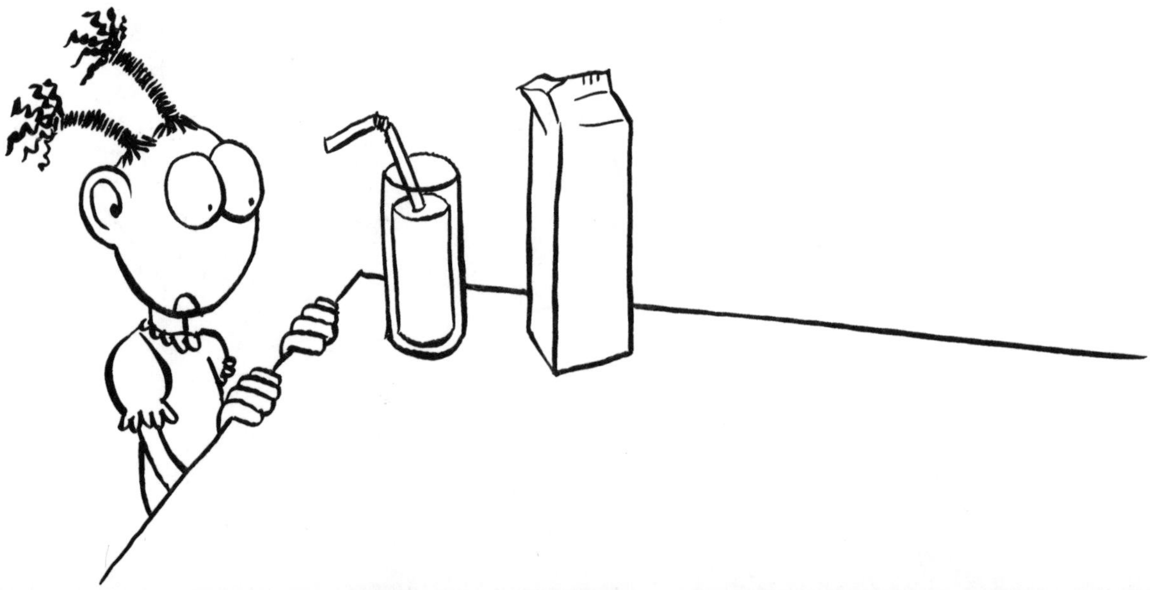

* A SLICE OF CHEESE WILL PLAY A SHORT FILM ABOUT COWS

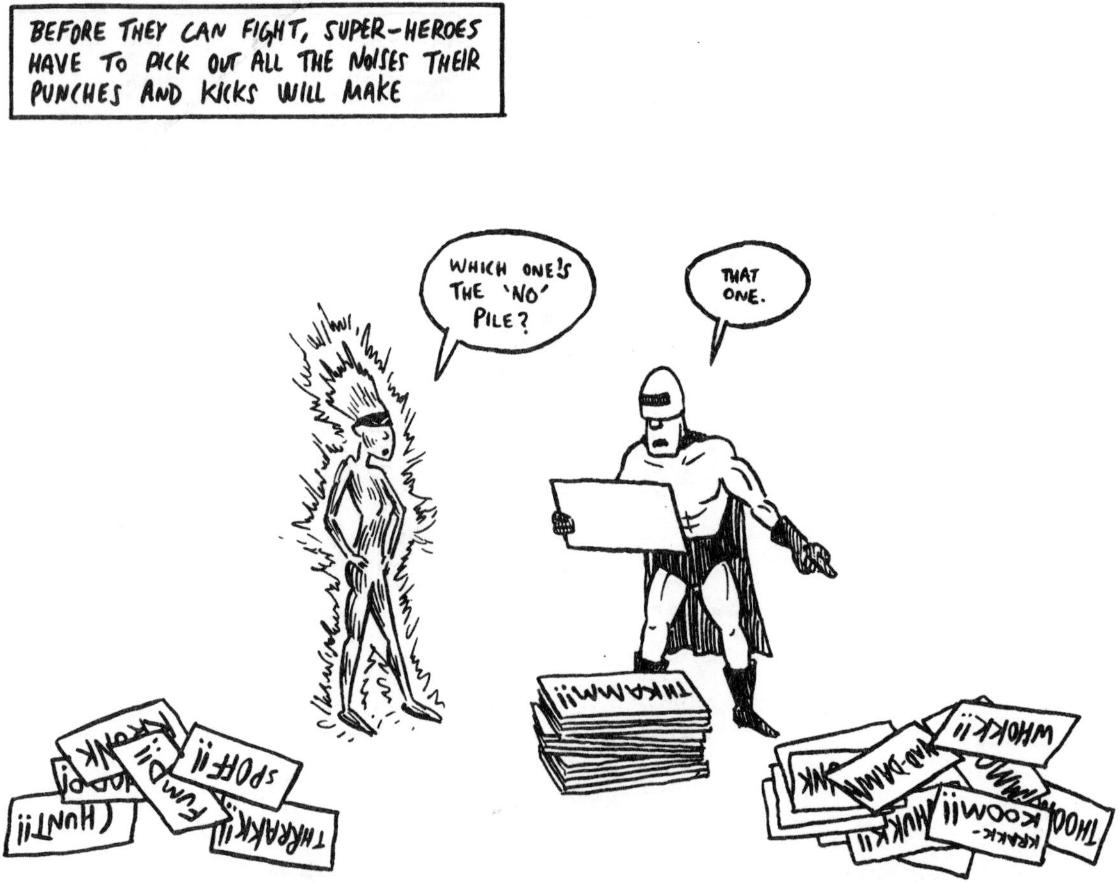
BEFORE THEY CAN FIGHT, SUPER-HEROES HAVE TO PICK OUT ALL THE NOISES THEIR PUNCHES AND KICKS WILL MAKE
WHICH ONE'S THE 'NO' PILE?
THAT ONE.

STRICTLY SPEAKING, THE TOMATO
IS NOT A VEGETABLE

IT'S REALLY A KIND OF DOLPHIN

THERE'S A DIRECTOR'S CUT OF "THE SOUND OF MUSIC" WITH A DIFFERENT ENDING

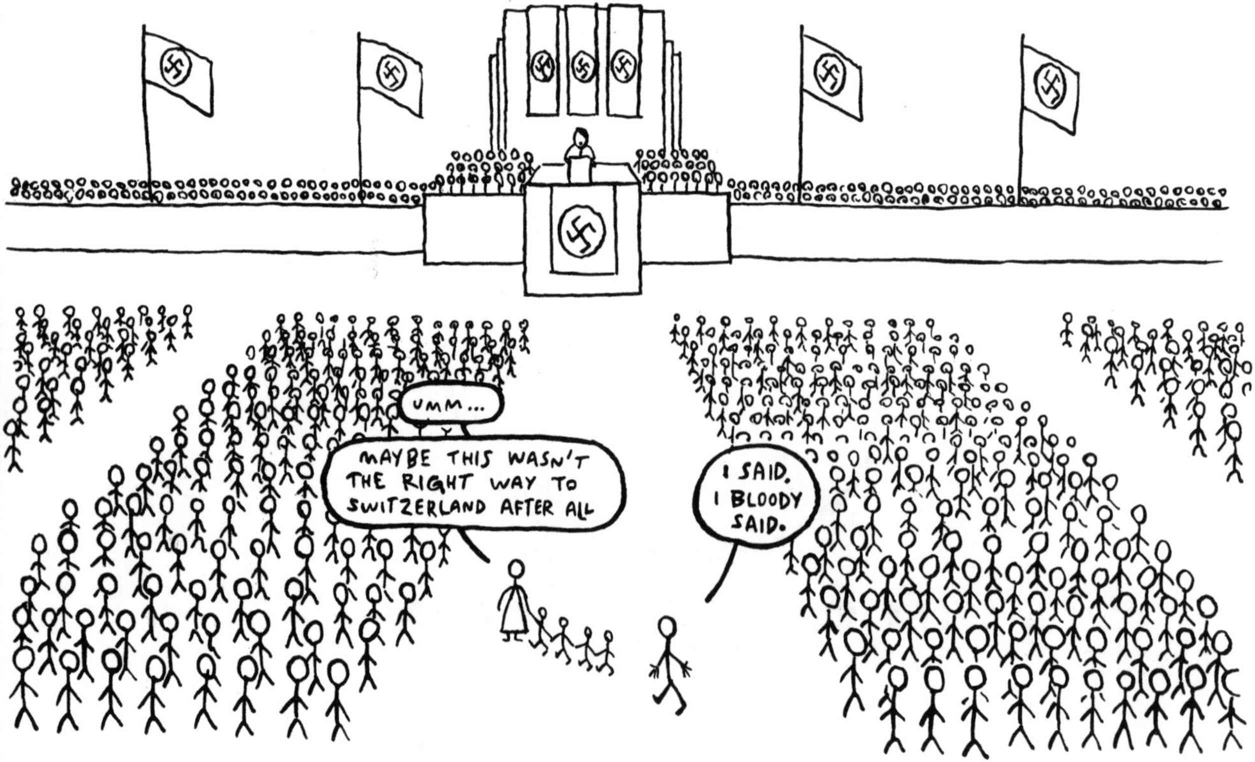
UMM...
MAYBE THIS WASN'T THE RIGHT WAY TO SWITZERLAND AFTER ALL
I SAID. I BLOODY SAID.

THE CAN OPENER WAS
INVENTED 98 YEARS
BEFORE THE CAN

ONE IN TEN FISH ARE AFRAID OF WATER

LIONS CARRY BARCODE SCANNERS

THEY RUN THEM OVER ZEBRAS TO CHECK HOW
MUCH THEY COST BEFORE THEY EAT THEM

MEN DON'T GO BALD NATURALLY

THEY JUST LIKE GETTING THEIR HAIR CUT THAT WAY

the victorians forgot to have the year 1862

> the error went unnoticed for more than a century
> the year was finally held between 1995 and 1996

MICE COLLECT YOUR DANDRUFF
AND EAT IT AS CORNFLAKES

THIS SQUARE HAS A SECRET
FIFTH SIDE WHICH YOU WILL
ONLY SEE IF YOU STARE
AT IT FOR A VERY VERY
VERY LONG TIME

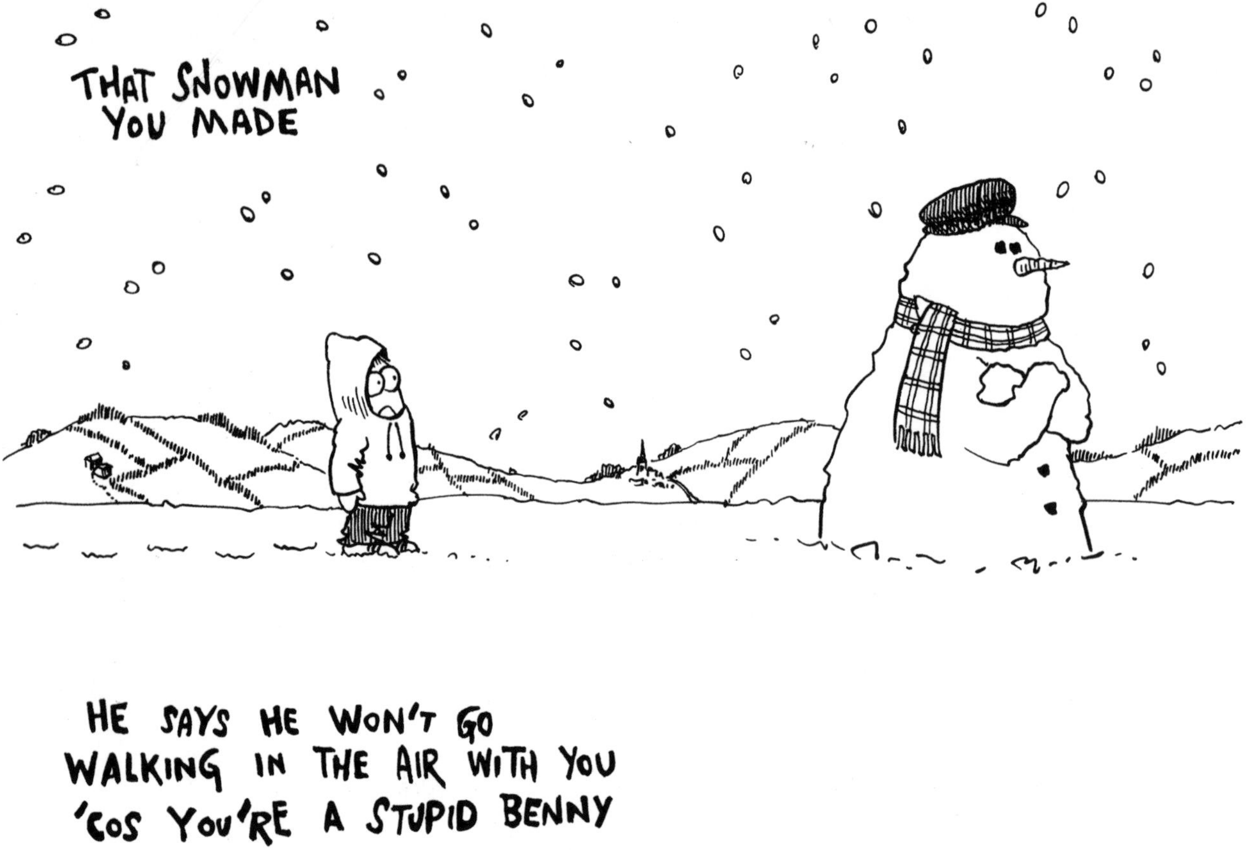
THAT SNOWMAN YOU MADE
HE SAYS HE WON'T GO WALKING IN THE AIR WITH YOU 'COS YOU'RE A STUPID BENNY

SCATTER DRAWING PINS NEXT TO AN ANTS' NEST
THEN WAIT TILL IT RAINS
THEY'LL PICK THEM UP AND USE THEM AS UMBRELLAS

BAR CODES WERE SIMPLER IN THE OLD DAYS

CLOWNS MELT AT 85°F

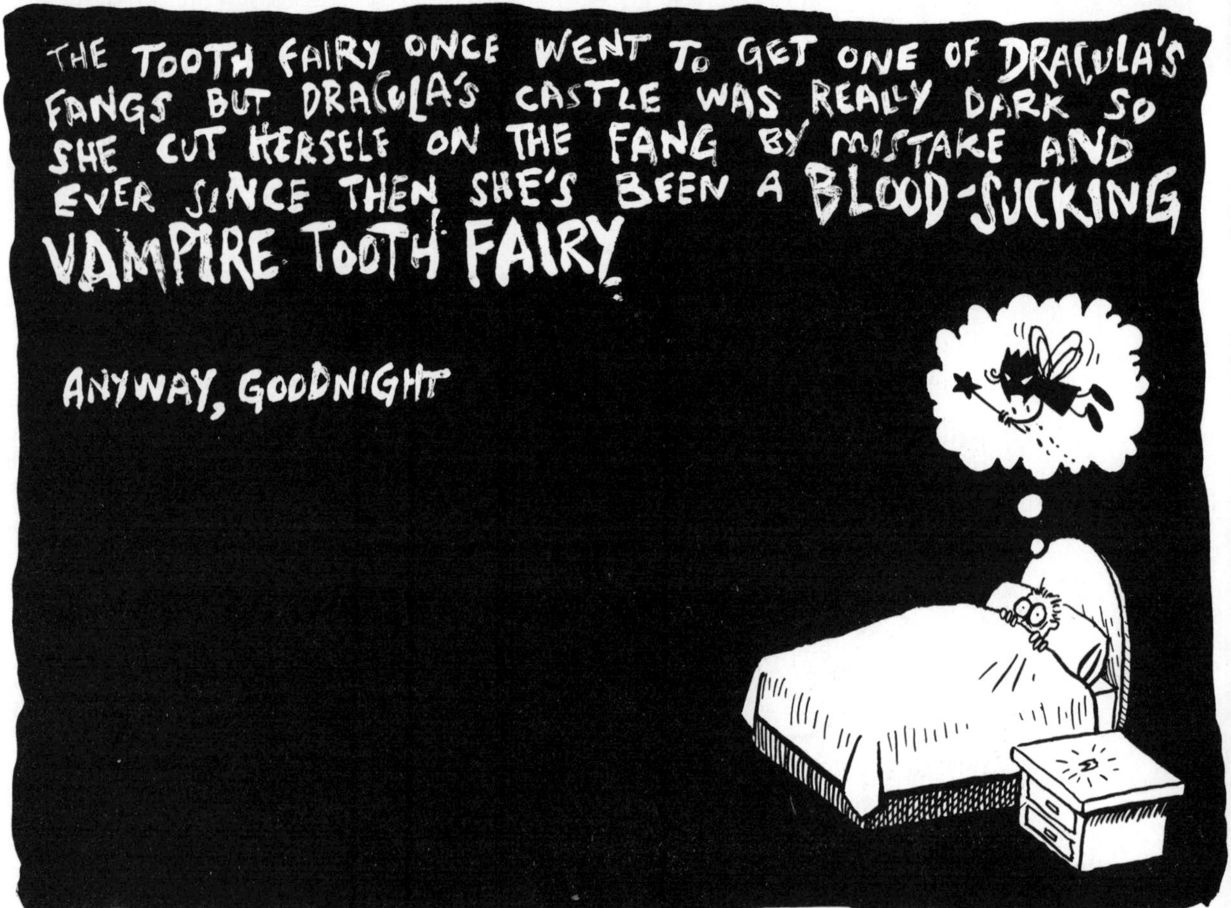
THE TOOTH FAIRY ONCE WENT TO GET ONE OF DRACULA'S FANGS BUT DRACULA'S CASTLE WAS REALLY DARK SO SHE CUT HERSELF ON THE FANG BY MISTAKE AND EVER SINCE THEN SHE'S BEEN A BLOOD-SUCKING VAMPIRE TOOTH FAIRY
ANYWAY, GOODNIGHT

THAT WORD DAD
USES SOMETIMES

IT MEANS "PLEASE"

USE IT IN SCHOOL
AND AT THE SHOPS

MUGS ARE JUST CUPS WHO'VE BEEN TO THE GYM

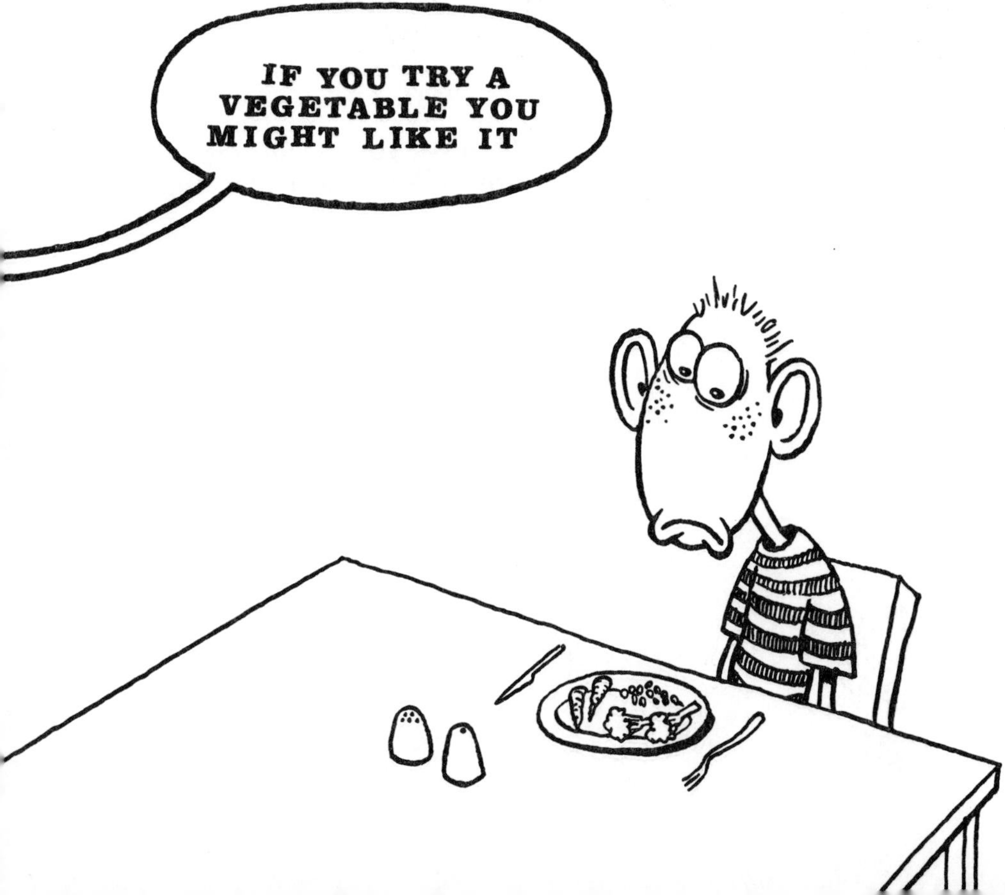
IF YOU TRY A VEGETABLE YOU MIGHT LIKE IT

they say no two snowflakes are the same
but who's ever checked?
i'll give you a hundred dollars
if you find me a matching pair

penguins spend a lot of time wondering why pixar have never made a movie about them

GODZILLA HAS EVERY FRIDAY OFF

ALL WIND IS MADE BY WIND FARMS

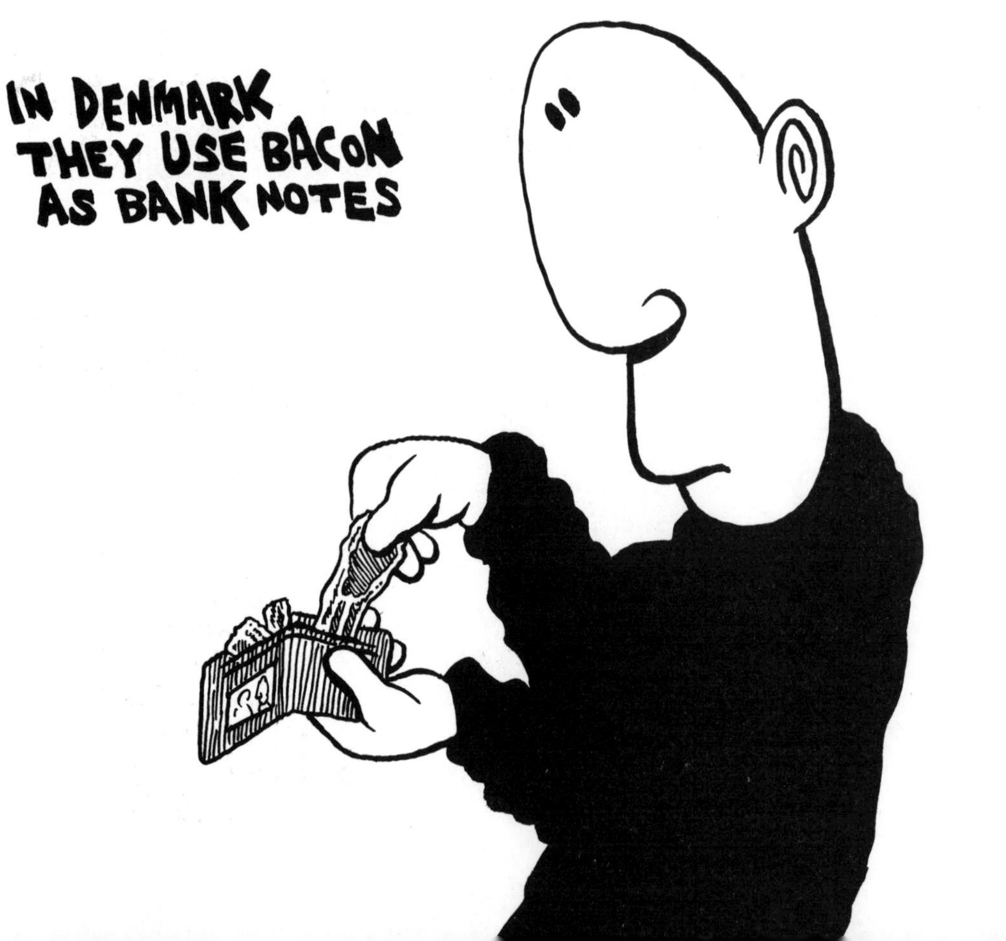
IN DENMARK
THEY USE BACON
AS BANK NOTES

BEWARE OF GUITARS

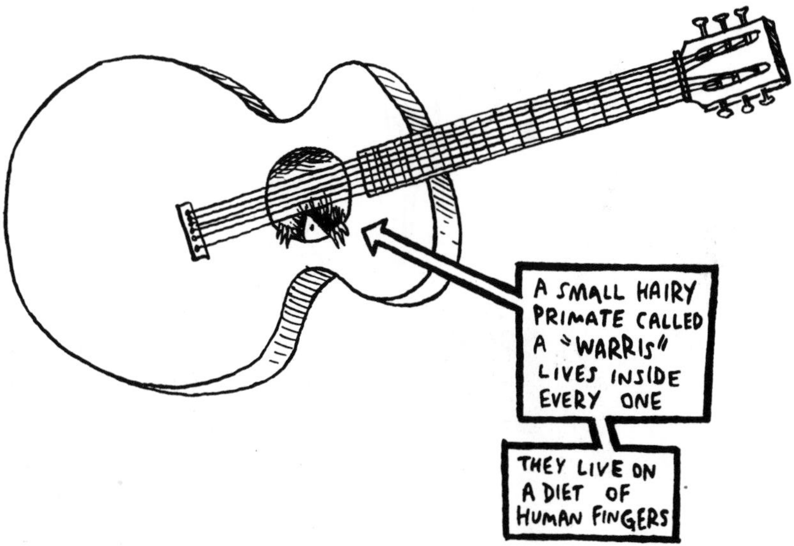
A SMALL HAIRY PRIMATE CALLED A "WARRIS" LIVES INSIDE EVERY ONE
THEY LIVE ON A DIET OF HUMAN FINGERS

IF YOU GRAB THE EDGE
OF YOUR CHAIR AND
PULL AS HARD AS YOU
CAN YOU'LL LIFT YOURSELF
INTO THE AIR

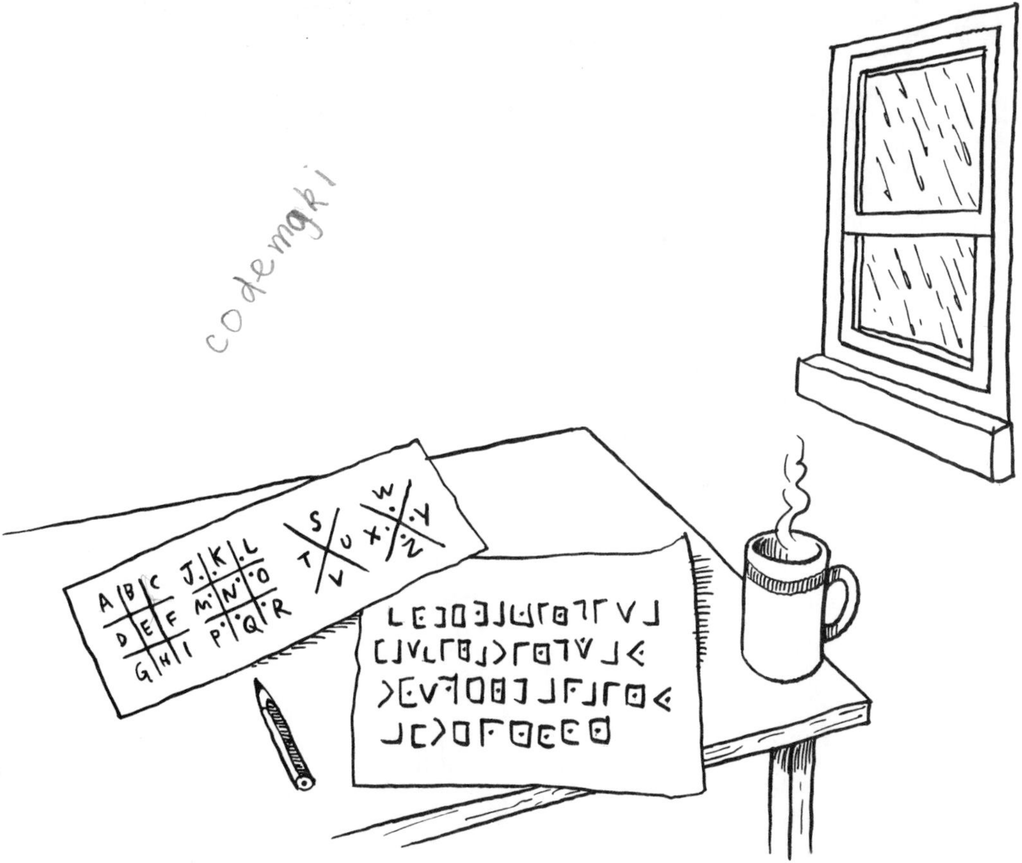
A B C
D E F
G H I
J K L
M N O
P Q R
S T U V
W X Y Z

IT WAS GRANDAD WHO BURNED ALL YOUR BARNEY VIDEOS

NOT US

PUBS HAVE SPECIAL
MAGNETS WHICH
DRAG DAD IN BY
HIS METAL FILLINGS

HE HAS NO CHOICE

THERE USED TO BE A SHIP IN THAT BOTTLE

BUT IT SANK

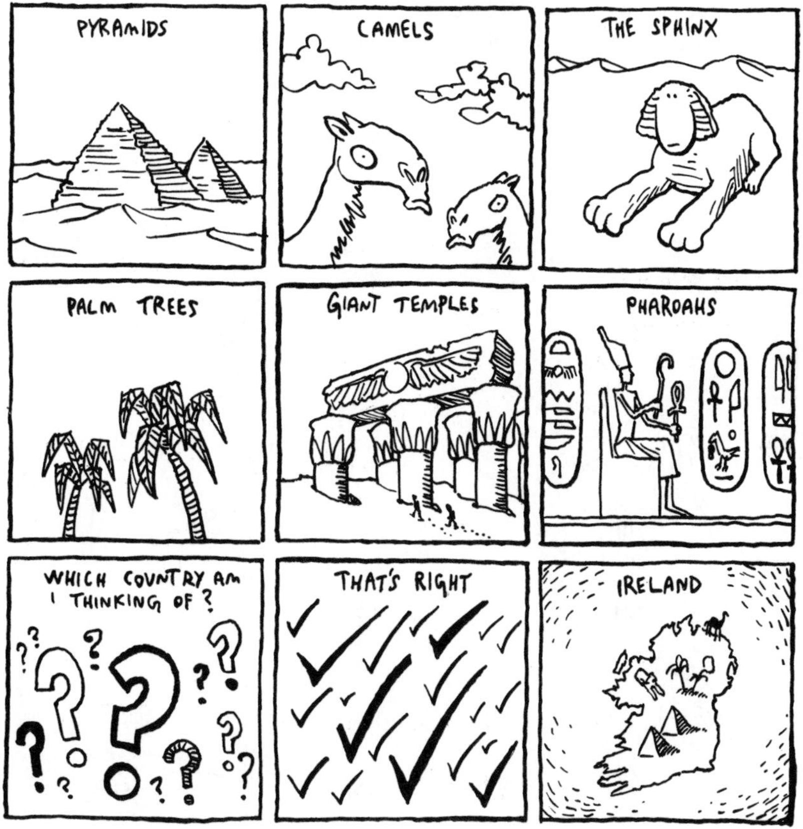

PYRAMIDS
CAMELS
THE SPHINX
PALM TREES
GIANT TEMPLES
PHAROAHS
WHICH COUNTRY AM I THINKING OF?
THAT'S RIGHT
IRELAND

YOUR DAD IS REALLY A YETI
HE SHAVES HIS ENTIRE BODY EVERY MORNING

before

after

"JACK"

CAPTAIN JACK WENDOVER
(1715 - 1763) LOST MORE
BODY PARTS THAN ANY
OTHER PIRATE IN HISTORY

TWO IN EVERY FORTY THOUSAND
CARS LEAVE THE FACTORY
AS "SIAMESE CARS"

IF THEY SHARE AN AXLE
THEY CAN NEVER BE SEPARATED

A NEW SUN GOES OVER EVERY DAY
THERE'S A BIG PILE OF THEM ON
THE OTHER SIDE OF THAT HILL

WHEN THEY COOL DOWN PEOPLE
CUT THEM INTO BLOCKS AND
THAT'S WHERE WE GET MARGARINE FROM

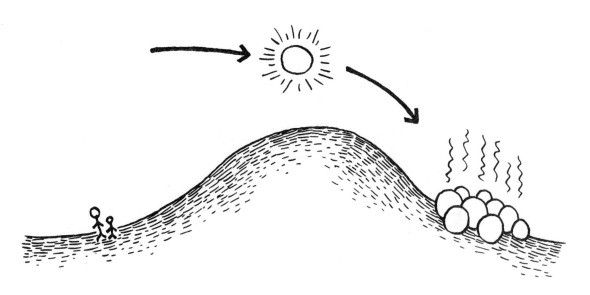

ONE IN EIGHT EARTHWORMS HAVE PIERCINGS
ONE IN TWENTY HAVE TATTOOS

MOST BIRDS WEAR PARACHUTES IN CASE THEY SUDDENLY FORGET HOW TO FLY

THE LAST VIKING RAIDS TOOK PLACE IN THE MID-1980s

eggs talk to each other after you shut the fridge door

THE WILD WEST WAS ONLY
TEN BY EIGHT FEET WIDE

SLUGS

are just snails who've
been mugged by other
snails

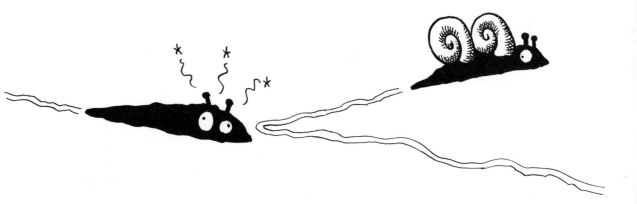

If you ring the number of a house where you used to live you can talk to THE PAST VERSION OF YOURSELF

Never tell the THE PAST VERSION OF YOURSELF who is calling

NOTE: anyone who rings you and says 'sorry, wrong number' is almost certainly you from the future

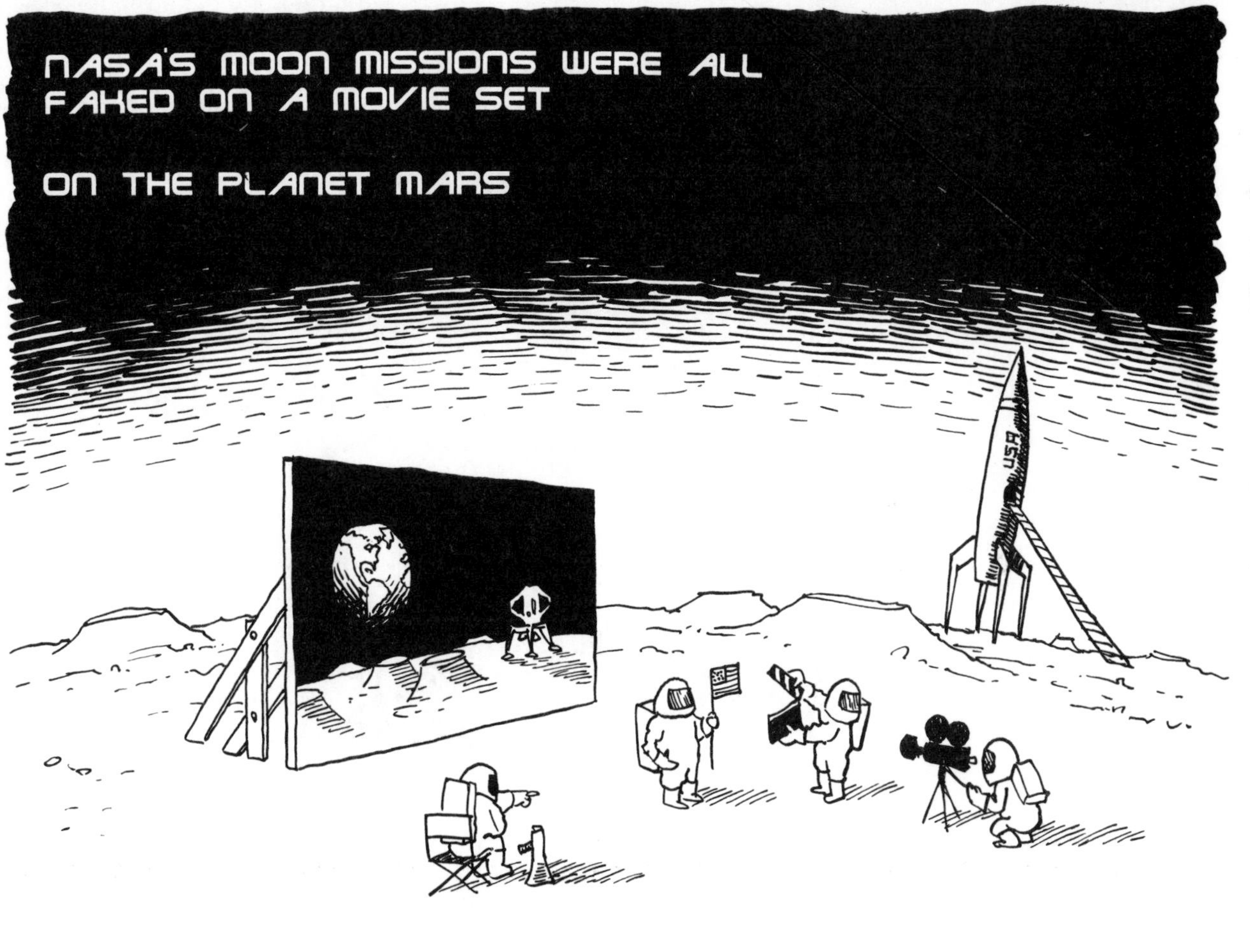

NASA'S MOON MISSIONS WERE ALL FAKED ON A MOVIE SET
ON THE PLANET MARS
USA

WE'LL GIVE YOU A PONY
IF YOU CLEAN
THE CAR

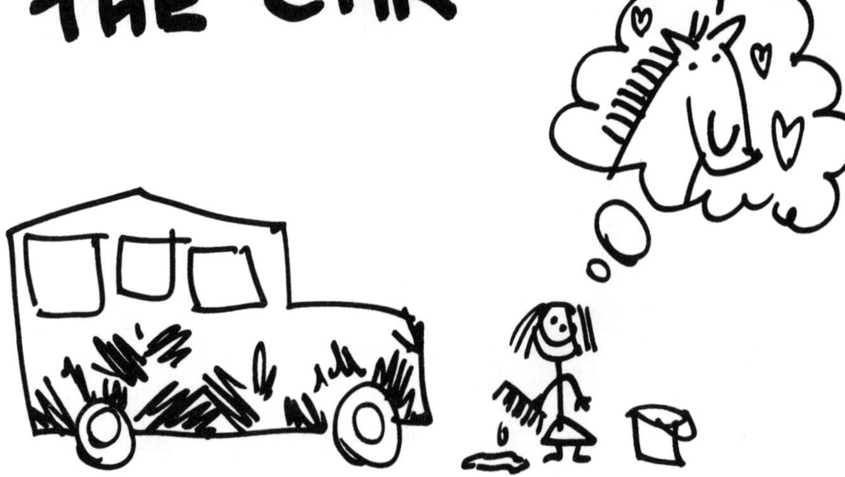

orange-hatted witches

always forget to
read road signs

KEEP A CHICKEN NUGGET IN A SHOE BOX, LEAVE IT SOME
WATER AND CORN, AND SOON IT WILL GROW INTO A LIVE CHICKEN

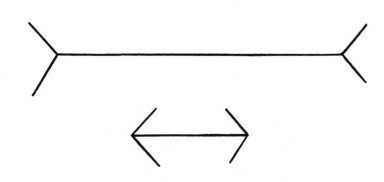

LOOK AT THE TWO HORIZONTAL
LINES ON THIS PAGE. **WHICH
ONE IS LONGER?**

THE CORRECT ANSWER IS
NEITHER. IF YOU THINK
THE TOP ONE IS LONGER THAT'S
JUST AN OPTICAL ILLUSION.

SAY A PRAYER BEFORE
YOU GO TO BED

THEN OPEN THE WINDOW
AND MAKE A RABBIT
SNARE

BY MORNING YOU'LL
HAVE CAUGHT A
REAL ANGEL TO
KEEP AS A PET !!

the statue of liberty switches hands when her torch arm gets tired
she only does it when no-one's looking

the next time should be in about twelve years

WHEN YOU REACH
TWELVE OR SO, YOU WILL
GROW PUBIC HAIR AND
YOUR SKIN MAY GET SPOTTY

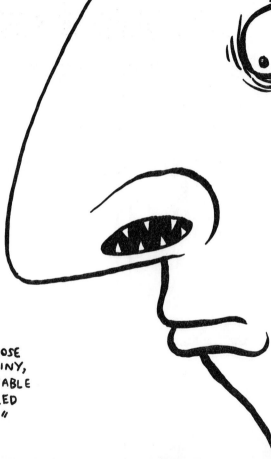

AND YOUR NOSE
WILL GROW TINY,
SHARP RETRACTABLE
TEETH CALLED
"DENTICLES"

YOUR DAD IS A SUPER-HERO

>He was bitten by a radioactive MAN, giving him all the powers of a MAN

>His super-hero name is 'MAN-MAN'

>His super-hero costume is jeans and a shirt from Gap

>His arch-nemesis is called 'All The Stuff That Needs Doing'

>Thrill to his exploits!

Q: WHERE DO BATTERIES GET THEIR POWER FROM?

A: TINY PEDALLING MICE

GOLDFISH CAN SEND
TEXT MESSAGES

DROP YOUR MOTHER'S
PHONE IN THE BOWL
AND YOU'LL SEE

IF YOU STICK YOUR
HAND DOWN THE
TOILET

IT COMES OUT OF
A TOILET IN
CHINA

TRY WAVING

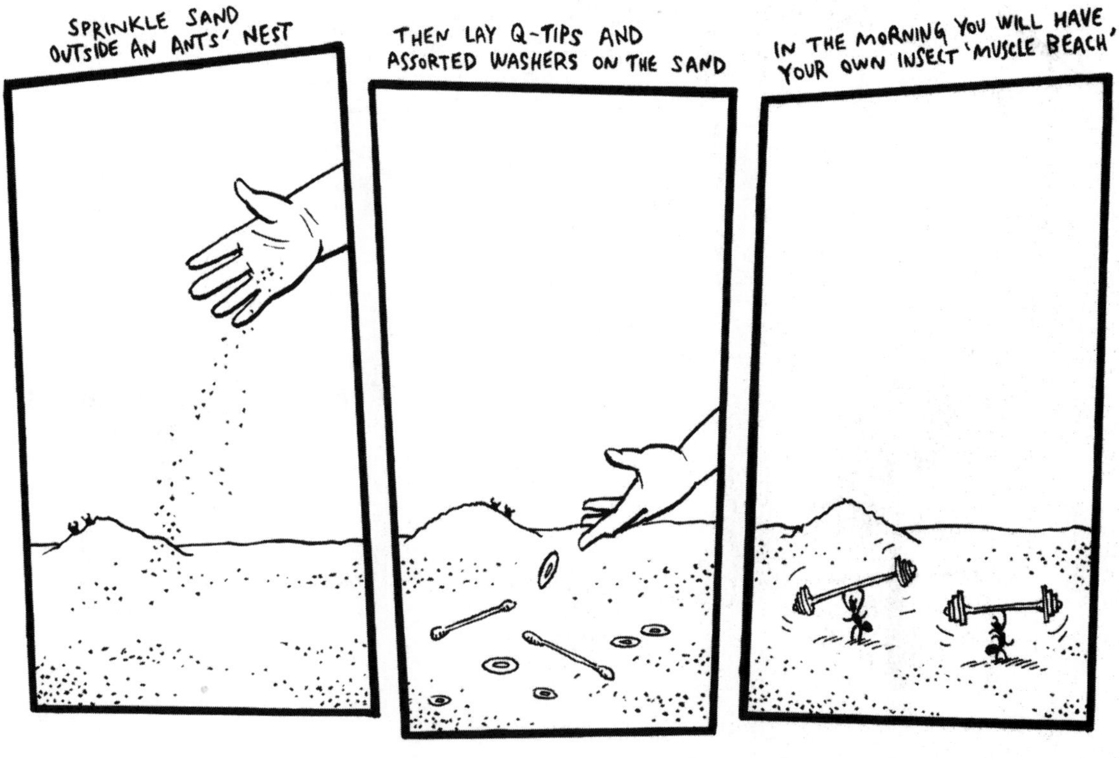
SPRINKLE SAND OUTSIDE AN ANTS' NEST
THEN LAY Q-TIPS AND ASSORTED WASHERS ON THE SAND
IN THE MORNING YOU WILL HAVE YOUR OWN INSECT 'MUSCLE BEACH'

THAT ROAD SIGN MEANS
"BE VERY QUIET
IN THE CAR"

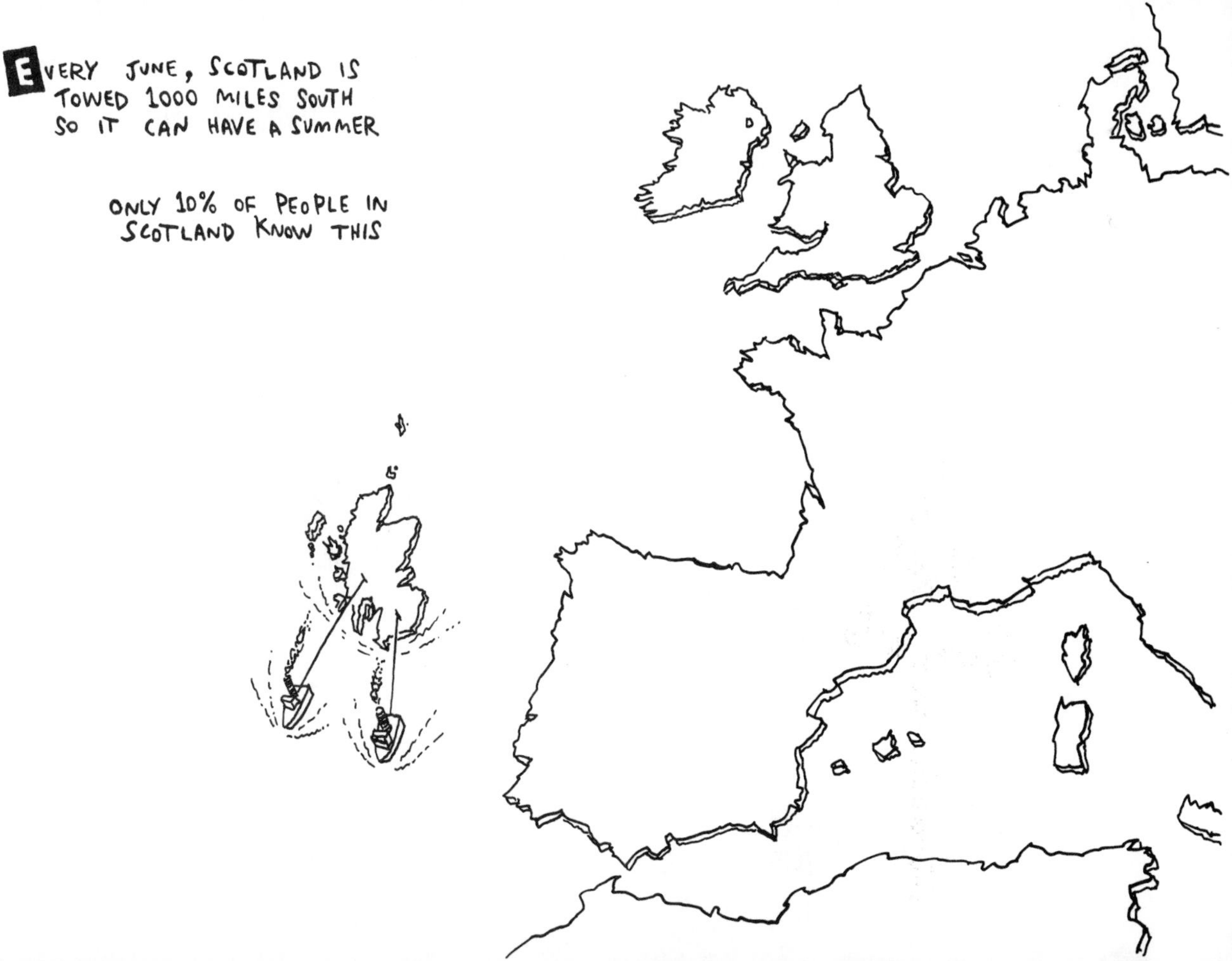
EVERY JUNE, SCOTLAND IS TOWED 1000 MILES SOUTH SO IT CAN HAVE A SUMMER
ONLY 10% OF PEOPLE IN SCOTLAND KNOW THIS

IF YOU UTTER THE TRIGGER WORD "BADMINTON"
TO YOUR GRANDMA

HER ORIGINAL PROGRAMMING WILL ACTIVATE
AND SHE WILL KILL ALL HUMANS

THE BEST COMPUTERS IN THE WORLD CAN BEAT ANYONE AT HUNGRY HUNGRY HIPPOS

EVEN RUSSIAN GRANDMASTERS

SANTA CLAUS IS IN HIDING IN THE
PAKISTAN / AFGHANISTAN BORDER REGION,
NEVER SLEEPING IN THE SAME PLACE FOR
TWO NIGHTS RUNNING

HE'S ON THE CIA'S TEN MOST WANTED LIST

SOME PEOPLE SAY DELTA
FORCE HAVE ALREADY KILLED
HIM

THEY DIDN'T STOP DAD FROM DRIVING
HE'S JUST GIVING HIS ARMS A REST

FOR TWO YEARS

ALL THE OTHER SHEPHERDS IN THE NATIVITY
PLAY ARE GETTING APPEARANCE MONEY

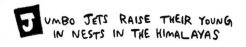 **J**UMBO JETS RAISE THEIR YOUNG IN NESTS IN THE HIMALAYAS

THE PARENTS FLY UP TO 3000 MILES TO GATHER NOURISHMENT FOR THE FAST-GROWING "JUMBLETS"

IT'S COMPLETELY IMPOSSIBLE TO
TOUCH YOUR OWN NOSE SO
DON'T EVEN TRY

CLOWNS ARE MADE PURELY
FROM THE CHEMICAL ELEMENT
"CLOWN" (SYMBOL Cw,
ATOMIC WEIGHT 15)

THIS IS AN ATOM OF
CLOWN MAGNIFIED
3,000,000 TIMES

HAMBURGERS IN THE WILD LIVE IN DESERT COLONIES

THEY HIDE UNDER ROCKY OVERHANGS TO AVOID COOKING
THEMSELVES IN THE HEAT OF THE DAY

LEAVE A FEW BOXES OF MATCHES AND SOME DRAWING PINS OUTSIDE AN ANTS' NEST

BY THE NEXT MORNING THEY'LL HAVE SET UP A RICKSHAW BUSINESS FOR SNAILS

THEY'RE NATURAL ENTREPRENEURS, ARE ANTS

WHEN SOMEONE SHAVES OFF A BEARD
IT GOES TO BEARD HEAVEN

ALL BALLOONS HAVE A REFLECTION OF A WINDOW IN THEM *EVEN WHEN THERE IS NO WINDOW NEARBY*

people who wear scarves

are just trying to hide the fact that they've got
heads but no necks

THE FASTEST RECORDED 100 METER
TIME IS 4.8 SECONDS BY MIGUEL
PIÑON IN THE 2000 OLYMPICS

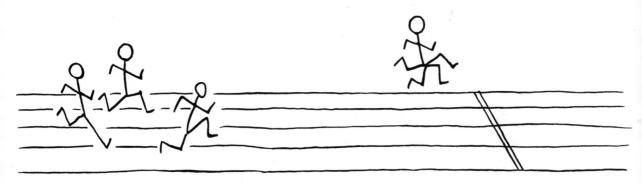

HIS MEDAL WAS LATER CONFISCATED AFTER
A RANDOM TEST SHOWED UP AN ILLEGAL
NUMBER OF LEGS

> CAT POOs ARE WORTH $300 EACH
> COLLECT THEM WITH TONGS
> WHEN YOU'VE GOT FIFTY, TAKE THEM TO THE
   POST OFFICE AND CLAIM YOUR MONEY

YOU KNOW MY MUG IN THE KITCHEN? THE ONE THAT SAYS

THERE ARE
ONLY THREE
IN EXISTENCE

THEY ARE
AWARDED
JUST ONCE
EVERY 100
YEARS

KNOW YOU DIDN'T SEE ANY GHOSTS WHEN WE VISITED THE CASTLE

THAT'S BECAUSE THEY WERE ALL ON THEIR CIGARETTE BREAK

WE DIDN'T HAVE I-PODS WHEN I WAS YOUR AGE

SO WE ALL HAD 20 PIECE MARCHING BANDS
WITH 10,000 SONGS MEMORIZED

if you spin round really fast and then stop your face will skid round to the back of your head

IF YOU BREAK THE LAW OF GRAVITY THE PENALTY IS HANGING

sometimes a daddy mole and a mummy giraffe have babies

though it's generally discouraged

THERE:

I'VE
DONE
YOU
AS
SPIDERMAN

THE END

NOW GO AND PLAY NICELY
AND NEVER EVER TELL FIBS